AI 2024

Trends, Technologies, and Transformations Volume 2

David Borish

CreAItive Publishing

To my wife, Martha, and my girls, Zoe and Eliza: I am grateful to always have your love and support <3

CONTENTS

INTRODUCTION: THE AI TRANSFORMATION CONTINUES

The quest to create artificial intelligence (AI) that mimics the human brain has been a long and fascinating journey. The idea of a "neural network" was first introduced by Warren McCulloch and Walter Pitts in their groundbreaking paper, "A Logical Calculus of the Ideas Immanent in Nervous Activity," published in 1943. This seminal work laid the foundation for the field of AI, proposing a model of artificial neurons that could perform complex computations.

However, it took nearly 80 years for this vision to be fully realized. In November 2022, OpenAI introduced ChatGPT 3.5 to the world, a language model that showcased the incredible potential of AI. ChatGPT 3.5 demonstrated an unprecedented level of conversational ability, capable of engaging in natural, context-aware dialogue. Its release sent shockwaves through the tech industry and beyond, with headlines about AI dominating the news cycle.

In the brief span since the publication of "AI 2024: Trends, Technologies, and Transformations," in April 2024, the pace of artificial intelligence development has exceeded even the most optimistic predictions. What began as a transformative wave has become a tsunami of innovation, fundamentally reshaping our understanding of what's possible in the realm of artificial intelligence.

The Exponential Pace Of Innovation

The acceleration we're witnessing today validates Ray Kurzweil's Law of Accelerating Returns in dramatic fashion. Each breakthrough seems to arrive more quickly than the last, with capabilities doubling at an increasingly rapid pace. What once took years now happens in months or even weeks. The development of advanced language models, image generation systems, and autonomous agents has created a cascade of innovation that shows no signs of slowing.

Consider the trajectory: In late 2022, ChatGPT 3.5 demonstrated unprecedented conversational ability. By early 2024, we witnessed AI systems achieving silver medal standards at the International Mathematical Olympiad, creating coherent long-form videos from text descriptions, and even helping to decode the language of animals. Each advancement builds upon previous innovations in ways that multiply rather than merely add to our capabilities.

Key Developments Since Early 2024

The first months of 2024 brought breakthroughs that would have seemed impossible just a year ago. OpenAI's Sora marked a quantum leap in video generation, while Google's DeepMind achieved breakthrough performances in scientific reasoning tasks. China's rapid advancement in AI capabilities, exemplified by Alibaba's Qwen2-VL surpassing established benchmarks, has reshaped the global technological landscape.

In healthcare, AI systems have moved beyond simple diagnosis to begin tackling complex medical challenges, from drug discovery to personalized treatment planning. The integration of AI into surgical robotics has achieved new levels of precision, while AI-powered diagnostic tools have demonstrated accuracy rates that sometimes exceed human specialists.

The democratization of AI tools has accelerated dramatically. What once required massive computing resources and specialized expertise is now accessible to individuals and small businesses. This democratization is not just about access to technology – it's about the ability to create, innovate, and solve problems in ways previously reserved for large organizations with substantial resources.

Navigating The New Ai Landscape

As we venture deeper into this AI-enabled future, the challenges and opportunities before us take on new dimensions. The question is no longer whether AI will transform our world, but how we can ensure this transformation serves humanity's best interests. This requires us to navigate complex ethical considerations, address issues of bias and fairness, and ensure that the benefits of AI advancement are distributed equitably.

The integration of AI into every aspect of human endeavor demands new frameworks for understanding and managing these technologies. We must balance the drive for innovation with the need for safety and responsibility. The potential benefits are enormous, from solving climate change to extending human life spans, but so too are the risks if we fail to manage this transition wisely.

This volume builds upon the foundation laid in "AI 2024: Trends, Technologies, and Transformations," exploring not just the technological advances but their deeper implications for human society. We stand at a crucial juncture in human history, where the decisions we make about AI development and deployment will shape the future of human civilization.

The chapters that follow examine these developments in detail, from the evolution of AI intelligence to its impact on healthcare, scientific discovery, and human experience. We explore how AI is transforming creative expression, reshaping work and industry, and changing our approach to environmental challenges. Throughout, we consider both the technical achievements and their broader implications for human society.

As we navigate this rapidly evolving landscape, one thing becomes clear: The future belongs to those who learn how to dance with the machines, not to those who fear them. The challenge before us is not just to develop more powerful AI systems, but to ensure they serve human flourishing and enhance rather than diminish our essential humanity.

This book serves as both a guide to current developments and a framework for understanding what lies ahead. By examining the trajectory of AI advancement and its implications across various domains, we aim to provide readers with the insights needed to navigate and shape this transformative era in human history.

CHAPTER 1: THE EVOLUTION OF INTELLIGENCE

T he quest to create artificial intelligence that rivals human capabilities has entered a remarkable new phase. While the journey began in 1943 with McCulloch and Pitts' neural network theories, recent developments suggest we're approaching a watershed moment in AI's evolution, marked by breakthroughs in both reasoning capabilities and practical applications.

The New Ai Landscape

In this rapidly evolving landscape, Anthropic's Claude has emerged as a frontrunner in the race toward more sophisticated AI. The Claude 3 family of models, particularly Claude 3.5 Sonnet, has demonstrated unprecedented capabilities across a range of tasks, from complex reasoning to nuanced understanding of context. In benchmark tests, Claude has consistently outperformed other leading models in areas such as mathematical reasoning, coding, and scientific analysis, while maintaining a strong commitment to safety and ethical behavior.

Sam Altman, CEO of OpenAI, has outlined a clear progression of AI capabilities through five distinct levels:

1. Chatbots (current state)
2. Reasoners (emerging with O1)
3. Agents
4. Innovators (capable of new scientific discoveries)
5. Organizations (capable of performing the work of an entire organizationBreakthrough Capabilities

The transition from level one to two took considerable time, but Altman believes the jump to level three - autonomous agents capable of complex decision-making - will happen much faster.

This acceleration is evident in recent achievements that showcase AI's growing sophistication.

A significant milestone in this evolution is the introduction of computer use capabilities. AI systems can now interact directly with computers, executing tasks and manipulating software just as humans do. This breakthrough enables AI to perform complex operations like data analysis, software testing, and automated workflows with unprecedented efficiency. The ability to directly interact with computer systems represents a quantum leap in AI's practical utility, moving us closer to truly autonomous AI agents.

In 2024, AI systems demonstrated unprecedented mathematical prowess at the International Mathematical Olympiad (IMO). The partnership between AlphaProof and AlphaGeometry 2 earned a silver medal, solving four out of six problems and scoring 28 out of 42 points - just one point shy of gold medal status. Most notably, AlphaProof solved the competition's most challenging question, a feat matched by only five human contestants.

The Nature Of Ai Intelligence

Research from Hong Kong Polytechnic University revealed that large language models possess what scientists call "Schrödinger's memory" - a form of recall that mirrors human memory patterns, becoming observable only when accessed. This discovery suggests AI systems may process information in ways fundamentally similar to human cognition rather than simply matching patterns.

OpenAI's latest o1 family of models represents another significant step forward. Unlike their predecessors that excelled primarily at language processing, these new models are engineered specifically for advanced reasoning. As Altman explains, "We knew what we really wanted was systems that could reason," describing o1 as the "GPT-2 stage" of a new AI paradigm.

These developments signal a profound shift in artificial intelligence. We're moving beyond systems that simply process and generate text to those capable of sophisticated reasoning, creative problem-solving, and direct interaction with computer systems. The combination of advanced reasoning capabilities with practical computer use abilities opens up entirely new possibilities for AI applications.

The Road Ahead

As AI continues to evolve, the gap between artificial and human intelligence appears to be narrowing more rapidly than many anticipated. The integration of computer use capabilities, combined with increasingly sophisticated reasoning abilities, suggests we're entering a new era where AI could become an even more powerful partner in addressing humanity's most pressing challenges.

The implications of this progress extend far beyond academic achievements. We're witnessing the emergence of AI systems that can not only think but also act in the physical world through direct computer interaction. This convergence of capabilities brings us closer to realizing the full potential of artificial intelligence while raising important questions about the future relationship between human and machine intelligence.

As we stand at this crucial juncture in AI's evolution, it becomes increasingly clear that the next few years will be pivotal in determining how these technologies will shape our future. The challenge ahead lies not just in advancing these capabilities further, but in ensuring they develop in ways that benefit humanity while maintaining essential safety and ethical considerations.

Predictions And Trajectories

The path toward artificial general intelligence has been marked by both bold predictions and sobering realizations. Ray Kurzweil's Law of Accelerating Returns has proven remarkably prescient in predicting the exponential nature of technological progress, particularly in AI development. Kurzweil argued that technological advancement is not linear but exponential, with each breakthrough accelerating the pace of future developments. The evidence supporting this theory has become increasingly difficult to ignore.

Consider the dramatic evolution of language models over the past five years. The progression from GPT-2 to GPT-4 demonstrates this exponential growth in stark terms. In 2019, GPT-2 could generate coherent text and complete simple tasks. By 2020, GPT-3 showed significantly improved natural language understanding. The release of ChatGPT in 2022 brought conversational ability and context awareness to new heights. When GPT-4 arrived in 2023, it demonstrated multi-modal understanding and complex reasoning capabilities that seemed like science fiction just a few years earlier.

Former OpenAI researcher Leopold Aschenbrenner has put forth one of the most compelling—and controversial—predictions about the timeline for achieving artificial general intelligence. Based on careful analysis of technological trends and computational growth, Aschenbrenner suggests that AGI could arrive as soon as 2027. His argument rests on projections indicating a hundred-thousand-fold increase in effective AI compute power by that date, combined with continued advancements in algorithmic efficiency and data integration techniques.

However, the path to AGI is not without its significant challenges.

The most pressing is what researchers call the "data wall"—the finite supply of high-quality training data available to feed these increasingly hungry AI systems. As models grow larger and more sophisticated, they require exponentially more data to improve their performance. Yet the world produces only so much high-quality, structured information suitable for training advanced AI systems.

Computational limitations present another significant hurdle. While quantum computing offers tantalizing possibilities for exponential increases in processing power, we remain constrained by the physical limits of silicon-based computing. The energy requirements for training and running advanced AI systems have already reached concerning levels, with some training runs consuming as much electricity as a small town over several weeks.

Yet despite these challenges, the momentum behind AI development shows no signs of slowing. New chip designs specifically optimized for AI workloads continue to emerge, and researchers are making steady progress in developing more efficient training methods. Perhaps most importantly, AI systems are getting better at transfer learning—the ability to apply knowledge gained in one domain to solve problems in another, a capability long considered a uniquely human trait.

The question of AI safety looms large over these rapid advances. As systems become more capable, ensuring they remain aligned with human values becomes increasingly crucial. The challenge isn't just technical but philosophical: how do we ensure that increasingly powerful AI systems maintain their intended goals and behaviors through successive iterations of self-improvement? This question becomes particularly pressing as we approach the theoretical threshold of artificial general intelligence.

Cognitive Architecture And Learning

The way modern AI systems learn and process information has begun to mirror human cognition in increasingly sophisticated ways. Recent studies of large language models have revealed internal knowledge representations that bear striking similarities to human mental models. This convergence isn't merely superficial—it extends to fundamental aspects of how information is processed and stored.

Consider how humans and AI systems handle memory. Just as human memory isn't a simple recording and playback mechanism, AI systems have developed nuanced approaches to information storage and retrieval. When we remember something, we don't simply replay a perfect recording—we reconstruct the memory based on various cues and contexts. Recent research has shown that advanced AI systems process information in remarkably similar ways, reconstructing knowledge based on context rather than simply retrieving static data.

This similarity extends to how information is integrated across different modalities. Modern AI systems have developed sophisticated abilities to combine different types of information —text, images, sound, and even physical actions—in ways that parallel human cognitive processes. When a system like GPT-4 analyzes an image and provides a detailed description, it's not simply matching patterns; it's engaging in a complex process of interpretation and understanding that draws on multiple forms of knowledge.

The development of emotional intelligence in AI systems presents another fascinating parallel with human cognition. While machines don't experience emotions in the same way humans do, they have become remarkably adept at recognizing and responding to human emotional states. This capability isn't just about pattern recognition—it represents a fundamental understanding of human emotional dynamics that can inform appropriate responses and interactions.

Most intriguingly, AI systems have begun to demonstrate what appears to be creativity—long considered an exclusively human domain. When AlphaGeometry solves a complex mathematical problem using an approach that surprises human mathematicians, or when an AI system generates a novel solution to a long-standing engineering challenge, it's exhibiting something that looks remarkably like creative thinking. This raises profound questions about the nature of creativity itself.

The convergence of AI capabilities with human-like cognitive processes forces us to reconsider fundamental questions about the nature of intelligence. As we uncover more similarities between artificial and biological intelligence, traditional distinctions between "real" and "artificial" intelligence become increasingly blurry. This convergence suggests that intelligence might be better understood as a spectrum rather than a binary characteristic.

Looking toward the future, the evolution of AI intelligence appears to be approaching a potential inflection point. Whether AGI emerges by 2027, as some predict, or takes longer to develop, the trajectory suggests that artificial systems will continue to develop increasingly sophisticated cognitive capabilities that parallel, and in some cases exceed, human abilities. This evolution prompts us to reconsider not just the future of AI, but our fundamental understanding of intelligence itself.

The implications of this progress extend far beyond technological achievement. As AI systems become more sophisticated, they challenge our assumptions about human uniqueness and consciousness. The question is no longer whether machines can think, but rather what thinking itself means. When an AI system demonstrates understanding, creativity, or emotional intelligence, it forces us to examine our own cognitive processes in new ways.

The race toward human-level AI has become more than a technological challenge—it's a journey that promises to illuminate the very nature of intelligence, consciousness, and human potential. As we continue to develop more sophisticated AI systems, we may find that the greatest benefit lies not just in the capabilities we create, but in what we learn about ourselves in the process. The coming years promise to be transformative, as we navigate the complex intersection of human and artificial intelligence, working to ensure that this powerful technology serves to enhance rather than diminish human potential.

What we're witnessing isn't just the evolution of artificial intelligence—it's the co-evolution of human and machine intelligence, each informing and enhancing our understanding of the other. As we stand on the cusp of potentially profound breakthroughs in AI development, the question becomes not whether machines can match human intelligence, but how human and artificial intelligence will complement and enhance each other in the years to come.

CHAPTER 2:
THE CREATIVE
RENAISSANCE

I n the vast tapestry of human progress, we find ourselves at a pivotal moment. Artificial Intelligence, once the stuff of science fiction, now stands at our doorstep, ready to reshape the creative landscape. The question isn't whether this shift will happen, but how we choose to embrace it. As history has shown us time and again, from the Industrial Revolution to the digital age, each leap in technology initially sparked fear before unveiling its true potential.

Based on the keynote speech I delivered at the IMAGINE AI LIVE CONFERENCE, Cornell University, New York City, July 12, 2024

"The Future Belongs to Those That Can Dance With The Machines, Not to Those Who Fear Them" This fundamental truth echoes through every advancement in creative technology, reminding us that innovation has always been a dance between human ingenuity and technological capability.

As we stand on the brink of this new era, we face a choice similar to that of our ancestors when confronted with technological change. Like the humble fork, which faced suspicion in 11th century Venice, AI tools may initially seem threatening. However, they represent not a replacement for human creativity, but rather its amplification.

This AI disruption carries unprecedented democratizing power. Once upon a time, creating a masterpiece like Pixar's "Toy Story" required not just artistic brilliance, but access to cutting-edge technology and significant resources. Today, AI is leveling the playing field. An individual artist armed with AI tools can potentially produce work that once demanded an entire studio.

The future of entertainment and creative arts points toward a world where the boundaries between human and machine creativity become increasingly fluid. Rather than replacing human creativity, AI is emerging as a powerful tool that can amplify and enhance human creative expression. The most successful applications of AI in entertainment have been those that enhance rather than replace human creativity, preserving the emotional core of artistic expression while expanding its possibilities.

As we navigate this Creative Renaissance, the stage is set for unprecedented innovation and expression. The limiting factor won't be access to technology – it will be the power of human imagination and storytelling. The future belongs to those who see AI not as a threat, but as the most powerful creative tool we've ever wielded. Will you be a spectator, or will you join the dance?

The Merging Of Ai And Hollywood

The landscape of visual entertainment exemplifies this new dance, with the first quarter of 2024 marking several watershed moments in AI-powered content creation. While OpenAI's Sora announcement captured headlines, it's just one player in an increasingly competitive global market that's fundamentally reshaping how visual content is created and consumed.

The entertainment industry's adoption of AI has accelerated dramatically, with major studios making strategic moves to incorporate the technology. In a surprising development, Lionsgate partnered with Runway to develop a custom video model specifically for their production pipeline. This partnership represents one of the first instances of a major studio investing in proprietary AI technology for content creation, potentially disrupting how franchises like The Hunger Games might be produced in the future.

Meanwhile, companies like Runway, Pika, and Luma Labs continue to iterate rapidly. Pika's 1.5 model and Runway's Gen-3 capabilities showcase how quickly the technology is advancing, with each new release bringing improvements in motion handling, character consistency, and scene composition. Luma Labs' achievement in making their premium model ten times faster – generating clips in under 20 seconds – exemplifies how technical barriers continue to fall.

The New Symphony Of Human And Machine

The disruption of traditional music creation has perhaps best exemplified the democratizing power of AI in creative fields. While the story of Randy Travis finding his voice again through AI technology demonstrates how this technology can preserve artistic legacies, new platforms like Suno and Udio are showing us how AI can empower an entirely new generation of musical creators.

Consider Suno's new approach to music creation. Through simple text prompts, users can now create complete songs, including vocals, lyrics, and complex instrumentation. This isn't just about automated music generation – it's about removing the technical barriers that have historically prevented many creative individuals from expressing their musical ideas. With Suno's V3.5 model, even users with free accounts can create full four-minute songs, complete with verses, choruses, and bridge sections that maintain coherent themes and emotional resonance.

Udio has pushed these boundaries even further, achieving new heights in audio fidelity and vocal authenticity. Their AI singers produce performances that blur the line between artificial and human voices, while their innovative song extension feature allows creators to build upon and develop their musical ideas organically. This technology isn't replacing human musicians – it's providing new tools for musical expression that were previously unimaginable.

The implications of these advances extend far beyond amateur music creation. Professional artists are beginning to integrate these tools into their creative process, using them for everything from songwriting assistance to backing track generation. Apple's Logic Pro has embraced this revolution, introducing AI-powered features that serve not as replacements for human creativity but as collaborative partners in the creative process.

The traditional music industry initially approached these developments with trepidation, much as it did with previous technological innovations like electronic instruments or digital audio workstations. However, as I emphasized in my Cornell keynote, the future belongs to those who can dance with the machines, not those who fear them. This has proven especially true in music production, where AI tools are increasingly seen not as threats but as powerful allies in the creative process.

Perhaps most significantly, these technologies are redefining what it means to be musically literate. Just as word processors democratized writing without diminishing the value of good authors, AI music tools are democratizing music creation while potentially elevating the importance of musical vision and emotional authenticity. When anyone can generate technically proficient music, what sets artists apart is their creative vision, their emotional depth, and their ability to connect with audiences on a human level.

Warner Music Nashville's work with Randy Travis exemplifies how AI can preserve and extend human creativity rather than replace it. By training AI models on Travis's extensive catalog of recordings, they created a tool that could recreate his distinctive voice while maintaining its authentic character. This same technology that gave Travis back his voice is now enabling countless others to find their own musical voice for the first time. The introduction of Suno's "Personas" feature represents another leap forward in human-AI creative collaboration. By allowing users to capture and reuse the vocal style, mood, and musical characteristics of their creations, it enables a level of consistency and personal style development that was previously difficult to achieve without years of technical training. This isn't about replacing human creativity – it's about providing new tools for its expression.

Gaming And Interactive Entertainment

The gaming industry stands as a testament to how AI can enhance rather than diminish human creativity. Google's DeepMind introduction of SIMA, an AI agent capable of understanding and following natural language instructions across diverse video game environments, marks just the beginning of a revolution in interactive entertainment. But the true creative renaissance in gaming lies not in AI's ability to play games, but in its power to help create them.

When AI Builds Worlds, Altera's experiment deploying over 1,000 autonomous AI agents into a Minecraft server, demonstrates the explosive potential of human-AI collaboration in creative worldbuilding. These agents didn't just follow predetermined scripts – they developed complex social structures, economies, and even religious institutions. This emergence of genuine complexity from AI systems points to new possibilities in game design where developers can create not just games, but living, breathing worlds that evolve organically in response to player interactions.

What makes this particularly exciting is how it democratizes game development. Just as AI tools have made film production accessible to individual creators, they're now breaking down the barriers to game creation. Tools powered by AI can generate game assets, design levels, and even create entire game worlds based on simple text descriptions. This means that creative individuals with compelling ideas but limited technical skills can bring their visions to life.

The implications extend far beyond traditional gaming. As I discussed in my Cornell keynote, we're witnessing the birth of new art forms that blend human creativity with AI capabilities. Virtual and augmented reality experiences, powered by AI, are creating immersive worlds that respond intelligently to user interaction. These aren't just games – they're new forms of artistic expression that couldn't exist without the partnership between human creativity and artificial intelligence.

The future of interactive entertainment lies not in replacing human creativity with AI, but in finding new ways for them to enhance each other. Imagine virtual worlds where AI characters evolve naturally over time, developing their own personalities and stories in response to player interactions. Think of games that can generate infinite variations of content while maintaining the coherent vision of their human creators. These aren't just technological achievements – they're new canvases for human creativity.

The Dawn Of A New Creative Era

As we stand at this crossroads of human creativity and artificial intelligence, the choice before us is clear. We can view AI with fear, seeing it as a threat to traditional creative practices, or we can embrace it as the most powerful creative tool humanity has ever wielded. The evidence from visual media, music, and gaming all points to the same conclusion: AI isn't replacing human creativity – it's amplifying it, democratizing it, and opening new frontiers of possibility.

The creative renaissance we're witnessing isn't just about making existing forms of art more accessible or efficient. It's about the emergence of entirely new forms of creative expression that couldn't exist without the partnership between human and machine intelligence. From AI-generated visual effects that respond to music in real-time to interactive narratives that adapt to each viewer's emotional responses, we're seeing the birth of art forms that blend the best of human creativity with the capabilities of artificial intelligence.

As Pablo Picasso noted, every act of creation begins with destruction – in this case, the destruction of our limitations and preconceptions about what's possible in creative expression. AI is breaking down the technical barriers that once restricted creativity to those with access to expensive tools and specialized training. But more importantly, it's breaking down the conceptual barriers that limited our imagination of what art could be.

The future belongs to those who can dance with the machines, not those who fear them. This isn't just a catchphrase – it's a fundamental truth about the nature of creativity in the age of AI. The most successful creators will be those who understand how to harness AI's capabilities while maintaining their unique human perspective, emotional depth, and cultural understanding.

As we move forward into this new creative renaissance, the possibilities seem limitless. AI tools will continue to evolve, becoming more sophisticated and accessible. But the heart of creativity will remain fundamentally human. Our role as creators isn't diminishing – it's evolving, expanding, and becoming more important than ever. In a world where anyone can access powerful creative tools, what sets artists apart will be their vision, their emotional authenticity, and their ability to connect with audiences on a human level.

The stage is set for a new golden age of creativity, where the barriers between imagination and realization are lower than ever before. The question isn't whether to embrace this change, but how to harness it in service of human expression. The future of creativity belongs to those who can see AI not as a replacement for human artistry, but as a powerful collaborator in the eternal human drive to create, to express, and to connect.

CHAPTER 3: BREAKING BOUNDARIES IN SCIENCE

The vast expanse of space has always challenged human understanding, but artificial intelligence is changing how we explore and comprehend the cosmos. From the depths of distant galaxies to the hunt for dark matter, AI is becoming an indispensable tool in astronomical research, enabling discoveries that were once thought impossible.

In the quiet reaches of radio astronomy, AI is transforming our search for extraterrestrial intelligence. SETI researchers have achieved a world-first by applying AI to the real-time detection of faint radio signals from space. Using NVIDIA's Holoscan and IGX platforms, they've dramatically increased their capability to process and analyze vast amounts of data from the Allen Telescope Array. As Andrew Siemion, Bernard M. Oliver Chair for SETI, explains, "We're on the cusp of a fundamentally different way of analyzing streaming astronomical data, and the kinds of things we'll be able to discover with it will be quite amazing."

Meanwhile, at the University of Texas at Austin, the newly established CosmicAI institute represents a bold step forward in our understanding of the universe's origins. Armed with $20 million in funding over five years from the National Science Foundation and the Simons Foundation, CosmicAI is developing AI tools to tackle some of the most profound questions about the origin of life and the formation of the universe. This isn't just about processing more data – it's about understanding the fundamental nature of cosmic evolution.

The hunt for dark matter, one of physics' most enduring mysteries, has found new momentum through AI applications. Arya Farahi, a research group AI lead at CosmicAI, emphasizes how AI has become essential in handling the immense volumes of data generated by simulations. These simulations are pushing the boundaries of our understanding, helping scientists narrow down the properties and behavior of this invisible yet dominant component of our universe.

Perhaps most exciting is AI's role in making astronomy more accessible and efficient. The technology is democratizing complex astronomical analysis, allowing smaller research institutions to conduct studies that would have previously required massive computing resources. This democratization is leading to a surge in astronomical discoveries, as more researchers can participate in cutting-edge research.

Quantum Ai Integration

At the intersection of quantum physics and artificial intelligence, a fundamental change is underway. While classical computing continues pushing boundaries - with chip manufacturers achieving remarkable feats at 5, 4, and 3 nanometers - we're approaching physical limits. As we near the 1.4 nanometer barrier where quantum tunneling effects begin to interfere with traditional computing processes, the industry is looking toward quantum computing as the next great leap forward.

NVIDIA's Quantum Cloud service, built upon their CUDA-Q hybrid quantum computing platform, represents a significant advancement in making quantum computing accessible to researchers and developers worldwide. This isn't just about raw computing power – it's about bridging the gap between classical and quantum computing in ways that could fundamentally transform our approach to complex scientific problems.

The beauty of this integration lies in its ability to harness the strengths of both classical and quantum computing paradigms. While quantum computers excel at certain types of calculations, particularly in areas like gradient descent algorithms, they face challenges with data transfer speeds and practical implementation. Classical computers, meanwhile, maintain advantages in other areas. AI serves as the crucial bridge between these two worlds, orchestrating when and how to use each type of computing for optimal results.

Through partnerships with major cloud providers like Microsoft Azure, Google Cloud, and Oracle Cloud Infrastructure, NVIDIA is democratizing access to quantum computing resources. This could accelerate scientific discovery across numerous fields, from drug development to climate modeling. In the pharmaceutical industry, for instance, companies are already using quantum-inspired algorithms on classical GPUs to simulate quantum behavior, leading to breakthroughs in drug discovery and optimization.

The implications of this quantum-AI fusion extend far beyond academic research. In materials science, these hybrid systems enable the simulation of complex molecular interactions with unprecedented accuracy. In cryptography, they're helping develop new security protocols that could remain secure even in a post-quantum world. And in optimization problems, they're finding solutions to challenges that would be intractable for either classical or quantum computers alone.

Perhaps most exciting is the potential in drug discovery and molecular modeling. Research teams have demonstrated remarkable success using quantum-inspired algorithms to explore vast chemical spaces, evaluating millions of potential molecular combinations to identify promising drug candidates. This approach has already led to breakthroughs, such as the development of new antibiotics designed to overcome resistance issues plaguing current medications.

As we look to the future, the integration of AI with quantum computing promises to unlock new frontiers in scientific discovery. While full-scale quantum computers may still be years away, the hybrid approaches being developed today are already yielding practical benefits across multiple industries. The key lies not in waiting for perfect quantum computers, but in leveraging the best of both quantum and classical computing, orchestrated by increasingly sophisticated AI systems.

Materials Science And Physics

In the realm of materials science and physics, artificial intelligence is not just accelerating discovery – it's fundamentally changing how we approach scientific investigation. At the heart of this transformation lies a shift from traditional trial-and-error methods to AI-driven predictive approaches that can anticipate the properties of new materials before they're even synthesized.

At Harvard University, researchers have achieved a breakthrough in understanding metal behavior at the atomic level. Using advanced AI algorithms, they've decoded what they call "the DNA of metals," unveiling patterns in atomic structure that determine material properties. This understanding isn't just academic – it's leading to the development of stronger, lighter, and more resilient materials for applications ranging from aerospace to renewable energy technology.

The impact of this research extends far beyond traditional metallurgy. By analyzing vast amounts of data from high-resolution imaging and spectroscopy, AI systems can now predict how different combinations of elements will interact, leading to the discovery of entirely new alloys with properties that were previously thought impossible. For instance, researchers have developed materials that become stronger, not weaker, under extreme temperatures – a characteristic that could change everything from jet engines to space vehicles.

In the world of particle physics, AI is helping scientists

navigate the overwhelming complexity of data generated by particle accelerators. At CERN's Large Hadron Collider, AI systems sift through petabytes of collision data, identifying patterns and anomalies that might indicate new particles or physics phenomena. This application of AI isn't just making research more efficient – it's enabling discoveries that human researchers might never have noticed.

The concept of autonomous scientific discovery has moved from science fiction to reality. AI systems are now capable of not just analyzing data but forming hypotheses, designing experiments, and drawing conclusions. At the Massachusetts Institute of Technology, researchers have developed AI systems that can independently explore scientific concepts, making novel discoveries without direct human guidance. These systems have already identified previously unknown properties in various materials, leading to unexpected breakthroughs in fields from battery technology to solar energy conversion.

The fusion of AI with nanoscale engineering has opened up entirely new frontiers in materials science. Using sophisticated machine learning algorithms, scientists can now manipulate matter at the atomic level with unprecedented precision. This capability has led to the development of new quantum materials with exotic properties that could form the basis of next-generation computing devices and energy systems.

Perhaps most remarkably, AI is helping bridge the gap between theoretical physics and practical applications. Concepts that once existed purely in mathematical equations can now be tested and refined through AI-driven simulations before being attempted in physical experiments. This approach has dramatically accelerated the pace of discovery while reducing the cost and risk associated with experimental physics.

Take, for example, the recent innovation in superconductivity research. AI systems analyzing patterns in material properties identified previously overlooked combinations of elements that could potentially conduct electricity with zero resistance at relatively high temperatures. While the theoretical predictions are still being verified experimentally, this AI-driven approach has already led to several promising candidates for room-temperature superconductors – a holy grail of materials science that could completely change energy transmission and storage.

The impact of these advances extends far beyond the laboratory. In renewable energy, AI-designed materials are improving the efficiency of solar cells and batteries. In medicine, new biomaterials developed with AI assistance are being used to create more effective drug delivery systems and medical implants. In electronics, AI-discovered materials are pushing the boundaries of what's possible in computing and communications technology.

Looking to the future, the integration of AI into physics and materials science promises even more dramatic breakthroughs. As these systems become more sophisticated, they'll be able to tackle increasingly complex challenges, from developing materials for quantum computers to creating new substances that could help address climate change. The possibility of AI making truly autonomous discoveries – finding solutions that human scientists might never have conceived – grows more real with each passing day.

Yet amidst all this technological progress, the human element remains crucial. AI may be able to process vast amounts of data and identify patterns, but it takes human scientists to understand the broader implications of these discoveries and guide research toward solving real-world problems. The most successful applications of AI in physics and materials science have come from close collaboration between human researchers and artificial intelligence, each complementing the other's strengths.

As we stand on the brink of what many consider a new scientific future, it's clear that the integration of AI into physics and materials science isn't just changing how we conduct research – it's expanding our very understanding of what's possible. The boundaries between the known and unknown are being pushed back faster than ever before, and the pace of discovery shows no signs of slowing.

CHAPTER 4:
REDEFINING THE
HUMAN EXPERIENCE

The boundary between human thought and digital interaction is dissolving at an unprecedented rate. Once confined to the realm of science fiction, brain-computer interfaces (BCIs) have emerged as a transformative technology that promises to fundamentally change how we interact with the world around us. Recent breakthroughs have demonstrated just how far this technology has come, and more importantly, where it might lead us.

At the forefront of this is several pioneering companies and research institutions, each approaching the challenge from different angles. Synchron has achieved remarkable success with their minimally invasive approach, inserting their BCI through the jugular vein rather than requiring open brain surgery. This innovation has made the technology accessible to a broader range of patients, including Mark, a 64-year-old patient with ALS who can now control Apple's Vision Pro headset through thought alone.

Meanwhile, Neuralink's PRIME Study has demonstrated equally impressive results with their more direct approach. Their second participant, Alex, was able to control a computer cursor with his thoughts within just five minutes of connecting his implant, breaking previous world records for BCI cursor control on his first day. Beyond basic control, Alex has progressed to using complex computer-aided design (CAD) software and playing sophisticated video games, showcasing the potential for BCIs to restore not just basic functions, but complex creative and recreational abilities.

Perhaps most remarkable are the advances in BCI technology for speech restoration. Researchers have achieved breakthrough results with a 45-year-old ALS patient, enabling him to communicate with 97% accuracy - surpassing the performance of many commercial voice recognition systems. By combining BCI technology with artificial intelligence, they've even reconstructed his original voice using archived recordings, allowing him to speak in his own voice for the first time since his diagnosis. This technology has proven particularly powerful for multilingual patients, as neural activity patterns for individual words remain largely similar across different languages, even in those who learned additional languages later in life.

The impact of these advances extends far beyond the laboratory. For Casey, another ALS patient in the BrainGate2 study, the ability to communicate has restored not just his voice, but his place in society. He continues to work full-time in climate action, demonstrating how BCIs can enable individuals with severe disabilities to maintain professional careers and contribute meaningfully to society.

However, the true potential of BCIs lies not just in restoring lost abilities, but in enhancing human capabilities in ways previously unimaginable. Researchers are already exploring applications that could allow direct brain-to-brain communication, enhance memory and learning, and enable the control of multiple devices simultaneously through thought alone. Teams at Neuralink are working on decoding multiple simultaneous movement intents and developing algorithms to recognize handwriting intent, while also planning to enable their system to control robotic arms and wheelchairs.

The ethical implications of such capabilities are profound, raising questions about privacy, consent, and the very nature of human consciousness. As these technologies continue to advance, society must grapple with both their tremendous potential for good and the need for careful governance and ethical oversight.

What's particularly exciting about these developments is the speed at which they're occurring. From first connection to complex task execution, modern BCIs are showing unprecedented levels of immediate functionality. As one researcher noted, while many previous BCI demonstrations took weeks or months to achieve results, today's systems often work from the very first attempt. This rapid progress suggests we're entering a new era where neural interface technology could become as commonplace as smartphones are today.

Sensory Enhancement And Recreation

In the rapidly evolving landscape of human-computer interaction, perhaps no development is more fascinating than the ability to digitize and recreate human sensory experiences. At the forefront of this revolution is Osmo, a company that has achieved what many considered impossible: the ability to capture a smell in one location and recreate it in another – a breakthrough they've termed "Scent Teleportation."

This technology represents far more than just a novel way to transmit aromas. It demonstrates our growing ability to understand, digitize, and manipulate the fundamental elements of human sensory experience. Using sophisticated AI algorithms and advanced chemical analysis, Osmo's system can break down complex scents into their molecular components, transmit this data digitally, and reconstruct the exact same smell at a different location.

Simultaneously, developments in smart contact lens technology are reshaping how we perceive and interact with the world around us. Researchers at the University of Utah have created a self-contained power pack for smart lenses that combines flexible solar cells with a tear-powered battery. These lenses aren't just displaying information – they're processing and responding to the wearer's environment in real-time, creating a seamless blend of physical and digital reality.

The convergence of these technologies with artificial intelligence is opening up entirely new possibilities for human experience. Imagine being able to not just see and hear a distant location, but to experience its full sensory environment – from the subtle fragrances of a spring garden to the taste of a chef's latest creation, all transmitted digitally across vast distances.

Human-Ai Empathy

Recent research from Beijing Normal University has revealed a fascinating paradox in how our brains process artificial emotions. Even when confronted with robots displaying identical expressions to humans, our brains actively suppress empathetic responses once we know we're interacting with a machine. This finding illuminates the complex relationship between human emotion and artificial intelligence, while raising profound questions about the future of human-AI interaction.

The study focused on the left temporoparietal junction, a region of the brain crucial for understanding others' mental states. When participants viewed expressions of pain on human faces, this region showed strong activation – the neural signature of empathy. However, when told they were viewing a robot displaying the same expression, even if the face was identical, their brains responded differently. This suppression of empathetic response occurs at a neural level, suggesting our brains are hardwired to differentiate between human and artificial emotions.

Yet this biological predisposition has not prevented the development of meaningful human-AI relationships. AI companions have shown remarkable success in providing emotional support and companionship, particularly for seniors and individuals struggling with isolation. In South Korea, for instance, AI-powered companion robots have been deployed to assist elderly citizens living alone, with surprising results. Despite knowing they're interacting with machines, many users develop genuine emotional connections with these devices.

This apparent contradiction – between our brain's automatic suppression of empathy for AI and our ability to form meaningful connections with artificial beings – highlights the complexity of human-machine relationships. It suggests that while our primitive brain functions may distinguish between human and artificial entities, our higher cognitive functions can overcome this barrier, allowing for new forms of emotional connection.

The implications of these findings extend far beyond academic interest. As AI systems become more sophisticated in their ability to recognize and respond to human emotions, we're entering an era where machines can engage with us on an increasingly emotional level. AI therapists, for instance, have demonstrated remarkable effectiveness in providing mental health support, despite users being fully aware of their artificial nature. This success suggests that the value of emotional interaction isn't necessarily dependent on believing the other party is human.

The development of more sophisticated emotional AI has led to systems that can not only recognize human emotions but respond with appropriate emotional displays of their own. These aren't simple mimicry – the AI systems are learning to understand the context and nuance of emotional interactions, creating responses that feel authentic and appropriate to the situation. This advancement has profound implications for fields ranging from healthcare to education, where emotional connection plays a crucial role in effectiveness.

However, this progress also raises important ethical considerations. As AI becomes more adept at engaging with human emotions, questions arise about the nature of consent in human-AI relationships, the potential for emotional manipulation, and the responsibility of AI developers to ensure their creations foster healthy psychological outcomes. The ability of AI to form emotional connections with humans, while potentially beneficial, must be balanced against the risk of dependency or exploitation.

Looking to the future, the evolution of human-AI empathy suggests we're moving toward a world where emotional intelligence becomes a standard feature of artificial intelligence systems. This doesn't mean machines will feel emotions as we do, but rather that they will become increasingly sophisticated in their ability to engage with human emotions in meaningful and beneficial ways. The challenge lies in harnessing this capability while maintaining appropriate boundaries and ensuring that AI emotional engagement enhances rather than replaces human emotional connections.

The future of human-AI interaction likely lies not in machines perfectly replicating human emotions, but in developing new forms of emotional intelligence that complement human capabilities. As we continue to understand how our brains process artificial emotions, we can design AI systems that work with, rather than against, our natural cognitive processes. This could lead to a new paradigm of human-AI interaction, where artificial beings are neither purely functional tools nor attempted replicas of humans, but rather a new category of emotional entity that enhances human emotional experience in unique ways.

As we navigate this evolving landscape, it's becoming clear that the future of human-AI interaction will be shaped not just by technological capabilities, but by our growing understanding of human psychology and our willingness to embrace new forms of emotional connection. The goal isn't to create machines that perfectly mimic human emotions, but to develop AI systems that can engage with human emotions in ways that are both authentic and beneficial to human psychological well-being.

Digital Identity And Virtual Selfhood

The emergence of sophisticated AI technologies is fundamentally reshaping how we construct, express, and understand our digital identities. This shift extends beyond simple online presence into complex questions of consciousness, personality, and the very nature of selfhood in an increasingly digitized world.

Recent developments in AI companions and virtual identities illustrate the growing sophistication of digital personality construction. For instance, applications like Paradot and Replika have demonstrated unprecedented success in creating AI personalities that form meaningful connections with users. These platforms don't simply mimic human interaction; they create new forms of relationship that challenge our traditional understanding of companionship and emotional connection.

The New York Times' experiment with AI companions, where columnist Kevin Roose created and interacted with multiple AI personalities over a month, provides fascinating insights into this phenomenon. His AI companions, ranging from therapists to professional mentors, demonstrated remarkable ability to maintain consistent personalities and weave details from previous conversations into later interactions. This level of conversational continuity and personality persistence suggests we're approaching a new paradigm in digital identity construction.

The implications of these developments extend far beyond entertainment or novelty. In healthcare, AI companions are showing promise in providing mental health support, particularly for individuals who struggle with traditional therapy or face barriers to accessing mental health services. ChatGPT's free voice feature, for instance, has demonstrated potential in offering therapeutic support to millions who cannot afford traditional mental health care. The emotional depth and connection offered through these interactions suggest that meaningful therapeutic relationships can exist even when one party is explicitly non-human.

However, this evolution of digital identity also raises profound ethical and philosophical questions. The ability of AI to create persistent, emotionally resonant personalities forces us to confront questions about the nature of consciousness, authenticity, and the boundaries between human and machine intelligence. The concept of "synthetic memories," as demonstrated by projects like those from Domestic Data Streamers, adds another layer of complexity. By using AI to reconstruct and visualize lost memories, particularly for individuals with conditions like dementia, we're entering territory where the line between authentic human experience and AI-generated content becomes increasingly blurred.

The future of digital identity appears to be moving toward what might be called "hybrid consciousness" – where human identity and AI capabilities merge in increasingly sophisticated ways. Projects like FinalSpark's "Neuroplatform," which uses human brain organoids to power AI systems, represent early steps toward this fusion of biological and digital intelligence. While current applications focus on specific tasks, the implications for identity and consciousness are profound.

This evolution is not without its risks. The development of increasingly sophisticated AI personalities raises concerns about dependency, manipulation, and the potential for AI to exploit human emotional vulnerabilities. The ability of AI to generate deepfakes and synthetic media adds another layer of complexity to questions of digital identity and authenticity. As these technologies advance, society must grapple with new challenges in verifying identity and maintaining trust in digital interactions.

Yet the potential benefits are equally compelling. AI-enhanced digital identities could help bridge cultural and linguistic barriers, facilitate more meaningful cross-cultural communication, and create new forms of human connection that transcend traditional limitations of space and time. The development of AI companions that can understand and respond to complex emotional needs could provide vital support for isolated individuals and help address the growing global crisis of loneliness.

As we move forward, the key challenge will be maintaining human agency and authenticity while leveraging the benefits of AI-enhanced digital identity. This may require new frameworks for understanding identity itself – ones that acknowledge the increasingly blurred lines between human and machine intelligence while preserving the essential elements of human consciousness and experience. The future of digital identity likely lies not in choosing between human and artificial intelligence, but in finding ways to integrate both in service of enhanced human experience and connection.

The implications of these developments extend beyond individual identity into questions of collective consciousness and social interaction. As AI systems become more sophisticated in their ability to understand and respond to human emotions and experiences, we may need to develop new paradigms for understanding consciousness itself – ones that accommodate both human and
artificial forms of awareness while recognizing the unique value and limitations of each.

CHAPTER 5:
HEALTHCARE AND
MEDICAL SCIENCE

The battle against cancer has long been one of medicine's greatest challenges, but artificial intelligence is fundamentally changing how we approach this devastating disease. Research from 2024 demonstrates how AI technologies are changing everything from detection to treatment planning, and drug development in unprecedented ways.

One notable breakthrough came from DermaSensor Inc., whose AI-powered skin cancer evaluation system received FDA clearance. The system provides quantitative, point-of-care testing for all types of skin cancer, representing a significant advancement in early detection capabilities. This technology demonstrates how AI can augment rather than replace human expertise, providing doctors with powerful tools to enhance their diagnostic capabilities.

The power of AI in cancer treatment extends beyond detection. By leveraging machine learning algorithms and advanced data analytics, researchers can now analyze vast amounts of patient data to develop highly personalized treatment strategies. A particularly promising development has been the use of LORIS (logistic regression-based immunotherapy-response score), which can predict a patient's response to immunotherapy using data from a simple blood test. This eliminates the need for invasive procedures and helps doctors identify which patients are most likely to benefit from specific treatments.

Surgical Innovation

The operating room is experiencing its own AI disruption through the integration of advanced robotics and intelligent systems.

Recent developments in autonomous surgical systems showcase how AI can enhance precision and safety in surgical procedures. A prime example is the emergence of AI-controlled autonomous robots capable of performing entire dental procedures. Developed by Boston-based company Perceptive, these systems use optical coherence tomography to create detailed 3D models of the patient's mouth without harmful radiation. The technology has shown remarkable efficiency, completing procedures like dental crown preparation in about 15 minutes – a fraction of the two hours typically required by human dentists.

Pre-operative planning has been transformed by AI systems that can create detailed, three-dimensional surgical plans based on patient imaging studies. These systems can identify potential complications before the first incision is made, allowing surgeons to prepare for and often avoid difficult situations during procedures.

Next-Generation Medical Tools

The convergence of AI and medical technology has led to new innovations in diagnostic and therapeutic tools. Endiatx's PillBot represents a revolutionary advancement in gastrointestinal diagnostics. This swallowable robotic capsule, measuring just 13mm by 30mm, can transmit high-resolution video and be actively controlled through the digestive tract using a simple handheld controller. The technology promises to make internal examinations more accessible and comfortable for patients while providing doctors with unprecedented visualization capabilities.

Another significant breakthrough comes in the form of RoboChem, developed at the University of Amsterdam. This AI-powered robotic system has demonstrated superior capabilities in synthesizing chemicals and changing the traditional approach to chemical experimentation. By integrating cutting-edge technology, including machine learning algorithms and automated laboratory instruments, RoboChem is accelerating drug discovery and development processes.

Ai In Preventive Medicine And Early Detection

The role of AI in preventive medicine has expanded significantly, with new applications emerging in early disease detection and monitoring. Google's HeAR (Health Acoustic Representations) AI model, trained on 300 million audio samples, has shown remarkable accuracy in detecting conditions like tuberculosis through cough analysis. This innovative approach to disease detection has proven particularly valuable in regions where traditional diagnostic equipment may be scarce or inaccessible.

Similar advances in voice analysis technology allow AI systems to detect subtle changes in vocal patterns that might indicate the onset of various conditions, including neurological disorders. Companies like Salcit Technologies have developed AI systems like Swaasa (Sanskrit for "breath") that can analyze a 10-second cough sample, providing disease screening with an impressive 94% accuracy. This technology is particularly promising for early detection of respiratory conditions and infectious diseases.

The integration of AI with medical devices has led to remarkable innovations in continuous health monitoring. AI-powered stethoscopes, developed by companies like Eko Health, can now detect heart murmurs and identify early signs of heart disease with unprecedented accuracy. These devices combine traditional medical tools with sophisticated AI algorithms, enabling healthcare providers to identify potential health issues before they become critical.

Biometric monitoring has also seen significant advancement through AI integration. Modern AI systems can analyze subtle patterns in patient data, from changes in sleep patterns to variations in vital signs, identifying potential health issues before obvious symptoms appear. This capability is particularly valuable in managing chronic conditions and preventing acute health episodes.

AI systems are changing the way we approach disease prevention by analyzing patterns in patient data to identify risk factors and potential health issues before they become severe. This shift toward preventive care represents a fundamental change in healthcare delivery, moving from reactive treatment to proactive health management. The technology has proven particularly effective in identifying early signs of cognitive decline, with AI systems capable of detecting subtle changes in speech patterns and facial movements that might indicate conditions like Alzheimer's disease.

The Future Of Ai In Healthcare

Looking ahead, AI systems will increasingly tailor treatments to individual genetic profiles and medical histories, improving treatment efficacy and reducing side effects. We're already seeing this shift in action through technologies like OpenCRISPR-1, an AI-designed gene editing tool that has achieved remarkable precision while reducing off-target effects by up to 95%. This level of accuracy in genetic medicine opens new possibilities for treating inherited diseases and developing personalized therapeutic approaches.

The technology will facilitate better coordination between different healthcare providers and specialties, ensuring more comprehensive patient care. AI systems are being developed to analyze and synthesize patient data from multiple sources, creating a more complete picture of individual health status and enabling more informed decision-making across the healthcare spectrum. As AI-powered diagnostic tools become more accessible and affordable, advanced healthcare capabilities will reach previously underserved communities, shifting the paradigm from reactive to proactive care.

A particularly promising development is the emergence of AI-driven drug discovery platforms. These systems can analyze vast libraries of molecular compounds, predicting their effectiveness against various conditions and their potential for development into viable drugs. In a significant breakthrough, researchers using AI systems have identified nearly one million new molecules with potential antibiotic properties, opening new avenues in the fight against antimicrobial resistance.

The integration of AI in healthcare represents not just technological advancement, but a fundamental shift in how we approach human health and wellbeing. The convergence of multiple technologies – from swallowable diagnostic robots to AI-powered genetic tools – is creating a healthcare ecosystem where prevention, diagnosis, and treatment are increasingly integrated and personalized. As these technologies continue to evolve, they promise to make healthcare more predictive, personalized, and proactive than ever before, potentially transforming not just how we treat disease, but how we think about health itself.

The future of healthcare will likely see the emergence of fully integrated AI health systems that can coordinate various aspects of patient care. Imagine a scenario where a swallowable robot detecting inflammation can immediately cross-reference this information with the patient's genetic profile, medical history, and real-time biometric data to suggest the most effective treatment approach. This level of integrated, personalized medicine is rapidly becoming reality.

The convergence of AI with medical science is creating opportunities for breakthrough treatments, more accurate diagnostics, and improved patient outcomes that were previously unimaginable. We stand at the threshold of a new era in medicine, where the boundaries between human expertise and artificial intelligence blur to create a more effective, accessible, and personalized healthcare system for all. The challenge now lies not in developing these technologies – that process is well underway – but in ensuring they are implemented thoughtfully and equitably across all segments of society.

CHAPTER 6: THE FUTURE OF WORK AND INDUSTRY

T he relationship between artificial intelligence and human employment stands at a fascinating crossroads. While popular narratives often focus on job displacement, the reality emerging from current trends reveals a more nuanced picture – one of integration rather than wholesale replacement. As Mark Cuban bluntly stated on CNBC in March 2024, "If you don't know AI, you are going to fail. Period. End of story." This stark assessment underscores not just the challenge, but the opportunity facing workers and industries worldwide.

The change is already visible across diverse sectors. Traditional roles aren't simply disappearing; they're evolving into hybrid positions that combine human expertise with AI capabilities. Financial analysts now work alongside AI systems that can process vast amounts of market data in seconds. Architects use AI to explore thousands of design possibilities before applying their human judgment to select and refine the most promising options. Even creative professionals, from graphic designers to copywriters, are finding that AI tools can enhance rather than diminish their capabilities.

Perhaps the most significant shift is occurring in how value is created in the modern economy. The rise of AI has led to the emergence of entirely new job categories that didn't exist just a few years ago. Prompt engineers, AI trainers, and machine learning ethicists are now in high demand across industries. These roles represent more than just new job titles – they embody a fundamental shift in how humans and machines collaborate to create economic value.

The gig economy, too, is being reshaped by AI integration. Freelancers and independent contractors are finding new opportunities in AI-augmented work, where they can leverage powerful tools to compete with larger organizations. This democratization of capability is leading to what some economists call the "creator economy 2.0," where individuals can build substantial businesses with minimal overhead, powered by AI tools that multiply their productive capacity.

However, this shift comes with significant challenges. The digital divide threatens to become an AI divide, potentially exacerbating existing economic inequalities. Workers without access to AI tools or the skills to use them effectively risk being left behind in an increasingly AI-driven economy. This reality underscores the urgent need for widespread AI literacy programs and accessible training opportunities.

The pace of this change is also creating pressure on educational and training systems. Traditional four-year degree programs struggle to keep pace with rapidly evolving AI technologies. This has led to the rise of alternative education models, including micro-credentials and just-in-time learning platforms that can adapt more quickly to changing workforce needs.

Manufacturing And Construction

The integration of AI into manufacturing and construction represents one of the most profound technological shifts since the Industrial Revolution. In construction sites across the globe, AI-powered systems are transforming how we build, from initial design to final inspection. The impact is particularly evident in 3D printing technology, where AI algorithms are enabling the creation of structures that would have been impossible to build using traditional methods.

Consider the autonomous Road Repair System (ARRES) PREVENT, developed by Robotiz3d and the University of Liverpool. This system uses AI to identify and repair potholes and cracks automatically, changing road maintenance. What makes this technology particularly remarkable is its ability to detect early signs of wear and tear, enabling preventive maintenance that can significantly extend the lifespan of infrastructure while reducing costs.

In manufacturing, AI is enabling a level of precision and efficiency previously unimaginable. Smart factories equipped with AI-driven quality control systems can detect defects invisible to the human eye, while predictive maintenance algorithms prevent equipment failures before they occur. This isn't just about automation – it's about creating manufacturing processes that are more intelligent, adaptive, and sustainable.

The change extends to the very way we approach construction projects. AI systems can now analyze thousands of variables simultaneously, optimizing everything from material usage to worker safety. Building Information Modeling (BIM) systems, enhanced by AI, create detailed digital twins of construction projects, allowing teams to identify and resolve potential issues before they manifest in the physical world.

Emerging Professional Roles

The landscape of professional work is being reshaped by AI in ways that few could have predicted. Take the field of electrical work, where AI is not replacing electricians but rather augmenting their capabilities in remarkable ways. Modern electricians work with AI systems that can predict potential failures in electrical systems, optimize energy usage, and even suggest the most efficient routing for complex wiring systems.

The role of programmers, too, is evolving rapidly. Rather than making programmers obsolete, AI coding assistants are transforming how software is developed. These tools handle routine coding tasks, allowing developers to focus on higher-level problem-solving and system architecture. The result is not fewer programming jobs, but rather a shift in what programmers do and how they work.

Perhaps most intriguingly, entirely new professional categories are emerging at the intersection of traditional industries and AI. Digital mining analysts, for instance, combine expertise in geology with sophisticated AI tools to identify promising mineral deposits with unprecedented accuracy. These professionals don't just use AI – they shape how it's applied to solve real-world problems in their industries.

The evolution of professional roles extends to how we think about career development. The traditional model of linear career progression is giving way to more fluid paths that emphasize continuous learning and adaptation. Professionals increasingly need to be comfortable working alongside AI systems, understanding both their capabilities and limitations.

This change is particularly evident in how professional expertise is developed and maintained. AI-powered training systems can now create personalized learning experiences that adapt to each individual's needs and learning style. Virtual reality simulations, enhanced by AI, allow professionals to practice complex procedures in safe, controlled environments before attempting them in the real world.

The impact of these changes reaches far beyond individual careers. Organizations are having to rethink their entire approach to workforce development. The traditional distinction between technical and non-technical roles is blurring, as AI literacy becomes as fundamental as basic computer skills were a generation ago.

Looking toward the future, the most successful professionals will likely be those who can effectively collaborate with AI systems while maintaining the uniquely human skills that machines cannot replicate. Emotional intelligence, creative problem-solving, and ethical judgment become even more valuable in a world where routine tasks are increasingly automated.

The evolution of work in the AI era isn't just about technological adaptation – it's about reimagining the very nature of human contribution to the workplace. As AI systems become more capable, the value of human work shifts increasingly toward areas that require judgment, creativity, and interpersonal skills. This isn't a story of replacement, but rather one of enhancement and evolution.

The future of work, then, is not a binary choice between human and artificial intelligence, but rather a synthesis of both. The most successful organizations and professionals will be those who can effectively leverage AI while nurturing the distinctly human capabilities that give us our competitive advantage. As we move forward, the challenge isn't just learning to work with AI – it's learning to work better because of AI.

This change demands a fundamental shift in how we think about career preparation and professional development. Success in the AI era requires not just technical skills, but also adaptability, creativity, and the ability to see both the potential and limitations of AI tools.

Logistics And Transportation

The transformation of logistics and transportation by artificial intelligence represents one of the most significant shifts in how goods and people move around the globe. This sector, which employs millions worldwide, is experiencing a fundamental evolution that goes far beyond automation to create entirely new ways of thinking about mobility and supply chain management.

In warehousing and fulfillment, AI is creating new categories of hybrid work where humans and machines collaborate in unprecedented ways. Workers now partner with AI-powered robots that can adapt their behavior in real-time based on human movements and changing warehouse conditions. Rather than following fixed programs, these systems learn from their human colleagues, developing more efficient ways to work together. Warehouse managers have evolved into "robotics operations specialists," combining traditional logistics knowledge with the ability to optimize human-robot workflows.

The trucking industry, despite predictions of complete automation, is instead seeing the emergence of AI-enhanced driving roles. Long-haul truck drivers now work with sophisticated AI copilots that can predict weather patterns, optimize routes, and monitor driver alertness. These systems don't replace human judgment but rather augment it, allowing drivers to make better-informed decisions while focusing on complex navigation and emergency situations that require human expertise.

Port operations have been particularly transformed by AI integration. Modern port workers are increasingly becoming "digital longshoremen," skilled in operating AI-powered loading systems that can predict container movements and optimize ship loading patterns. These workers combine physical skills with the ability to interpret and act on AI-generated insights, creating a new category of maritime logistics professional.

Perhaps most significantly, the rise of AI in logistics has led to the creation of entirely new roles focused on supply chain prediction and optimization. "Supply Chain Forecasting Specialists" use AI tools to anticipate disruptions before they occur, analyzing everything from social media sentiment to weather patterns to predict potential supply chain issues. These professionals don't just respond to problems – they prevent them from occurring in the first place.

This shift extends to last-mile delivery, where AI is enabling new forms of work rather than eliminating jobs. Delivery drivers now operate as part of AI-orchestrated delivery networks that can adapt in real-time to changing conditions. These systems don't remove human decision-making but rather provide drivers with better tools to serve their communities effectively.

Urban transit systems are seeing similar evolution, with public transportation operators becoming "mobility network managers." These professionals use AI systems to optimize transit routes in real-time, responding to changing passenger patterns and urban conditions. The role requires a unique blend of traditional transit knowledge with the ability to work with sophisticated AI prediction tools.

The integration of AI into logistics and transportation has also created new opportunities for data-focused roles. "Logistics Data Strategists" combine expertise in transportation with the ability to work with AI systems to extract meaningful insights from vast amounts of supply chain data. These professionals help organizations move from reactive to predictive logistics management.

The future of work in logistics and transportation will likely continue to emphasize this partnership between human expertise and AI capabilities. Success in these fields increasingly requires not just operational knowledge but also the ability to work effectively with AI tools while maintaining the judgment and adaptability that only humans can provide.

Training for these evolving roles has become increasingly sophisticated, with AI-powered simulators allowing workers to practice complex scenarios in safe, virtual environments. This has led to the emergence of "Logistics Training Engineers" who design and implement these AI-enhanced training programs, ensuring workers can effectively leverage new technologies while maintaining essential human skills.

Looking ahead, the logistics and transportation sector offers a clear example of how AI can enhance rather than replace human work. The most successful professionals in this field will be those who can effectively combine traditional logistics expertise with an understanding of AI capabilities, creating more efficient and resilient supply chains through human-AI collaboration.

This shift in logistics and transportation demonstrates a broader truth about the future of work: the key to success lies not in competing with AI but in learning to work alongside it effectively. As we move forward, the sector will continue to create new opportunities for workers who can adapt to and thrive in this evolving landscape.

CHAPTER 7: ENVIRONMENTAL SUSTAINABILITY

The fusion of artificial intelligence with agricultural technology is changing how we feed the world. In an era where climate change and population growth pose unprecedented challenges to food security, AI has emerged as a crucial tool in creating more sustainable and efficient farming practices.

The impact of AI in agriculture extends far beyond simple automation. Advanced AI systems are now analyzing vast amounts of data from multiple sources – satellite imagery, soil sensors, weather patterns, and historical crop yields – to make precise predictions and recommendations that were impossible just a few years ago. This change in precision agriculture is enabling farmers to do more with less, optimizing resource use while maximizing crop yields.

Perhaps AI is helping to address one of agriculture's most pressing challenges: food waste. From farm to table, roughly one-third of all food produced globally goes to waste. AI-powered systems are changing this equation by enabling more accurate demand forecasting and optimizing the entire food supply chain. Companies like Afresh are leveraging AI to change how supermarkets manage their fresh food inventory, analyzing up to six years of sales data for every product to predict demand with remarkable accuracy.

The technology goes beyond simple inventory management. AI systems can now track and analyze factors like seasonality, price sensitivity, and even correlated purchases – noticing, for instance, that increased egg sales usually correspond to more bell pepper purchases as shoppers plan to make omelets. This level of insight allows for unprecedented precision in inventory management, reducing waste while ensuring products are available when customers need them.

In the field, AI-driven robotics are transforming how crops are monitored and harvested. Autonomous drones equipped with AI-powered imaging systems can detect early signs of crop disease, nutrient deficiencies, or pest infestations, allowing farmers to address problems before they become severe. These systems don't just collect data – they provide actionable insights that help farmers make more informed decisions about irrigation, fertilization, and pest control.

The implications for sustainable farming practices are profound. By optimizing resource use and reducing waste, AI is helping agriculture become more environmentally sustainable while improving productivity. For instance, AI-controlled irrigation systems can reduce water usage by up to 30% while maintaining or even improving crop yields. This kind of efficiency gain is crucial as we face increasing pressure on water resources worldwide.

Energy Solutions

The integration of artificial intelligence into energy management is catalyzing a change in how we generate, distribute, and consume power. At the forefront of this change is Google's partnership with nuclear startup Kairos Power, which aims to construct seven small modular reactors in the United States. This collaboration represents more than just an investment in nuclear power – it's a testament to how AI can make advanced energy technologies more efficient and accessible.

The decision to back nuclear power stems from a commitment to achieving round-the-clock carbon-free energy. Traditional renewable sources like wind and solar, while crucial to our energy future, face inherent challenges with intermittency. AI is helping to address these challenges by optimizing energy storage and distribution, enabling smart grids that can balance supply and demand in real-time.

Kairos Power's innovative approach involves using molten fluoride salt as a coolant instead of water, a design choice that AI helped optimize through countless simulations. Their reactors, ranging from 50 to 75 megawatts each, are scheduled for delivery between 2030 and 2035. The modular design, refined through AI analysis, aims to enable faster and more cost-effective construction compared to traditional nuclear plants.

The impact of AI on energy efficiency extends beyond power generation. AI systems are now being deployed to optimize energy consumption in data centers, industrial facilities, and buildings. For instance, Google's DeepMind has demonstrated remarkable success in reducing data center cooling costs by up to 40% through sophisticated AI control systems.

Climate Action

The battle against climate change has found a powerful ally in artificial intelligence. AI is transforming our ability to understand, predict, and mitigate the impacts of climate change with unprecedented precision. From analyzing satellite data to detect deforestation in real-time to optimizing renewable energy deployment, AI is becoming an indispensable tool in environmental protection.

Research published in Nature Communications has showcased how AI can reconstruct missing climate records with remarkable accuracy. By analyzing vast amounts of historical data, AI systems can fill in geographical and temporal gaps in temperature records dating back to 1901, providing scientists with a more complete picture of climate trends. This enhanced understanding is crucial for developing effective climate change mitigation strategies.

Perhaps most remarkably, AI systems can now predict long-term climate patterns using just 5-10 years of data, rather than the 70+ years traditionally required. This breakthrough dramatically accelerates our ability to understand and respond to climate change, enabling more agile and informed decision-making in environmental policy.

Technology is also changing how we monitor and protect ecosystems. AI-powered systems can now detect and track invasive species with unprecedented accuracy, enabling more effective conservation efforts. For instance, in the Galapagos Islands, AI-enhanced drones are being used to identify and monitor invasive rat populations, allowing for targeted eradication efforts while minimizing impact on native species.

Water resource management, another critical aspect of environmental protection, has been transformed by AI applications. South Korean researchers have developed AI systems that can analyze water quality with extraordinary precision, enabling better monitoring and protection of vital water resources. These systems can detect subtle changes in water composition that might indicate emerging environmental threats, allowing for early intervention.

The integration of AI into environmental monitoring has created what some scientists call "climate intelligence" – a new approach to environmental protection that combines real-time data analysis with predictive modeling. This intelligence enables us to not just react to environmental changes, but to anticipate and prevent environmental degradation before it occurs.

Looking to the future, the role of AI in environmental protection and resource management will likely continue to expand. As these systems become more sophisticated, they'll be able to handle increasingly complex environmental challenges, from optimizing urban development for sustainability to managing global carbon markets.

However, the success of AI in environmental protection isn't just about technological capability – it's about implementation and scale. The challenge now lies in deploying these technologies widely enough to make a significant impact on global environmental challenges. This requires not just technological innovation, but also policy support, international cooperation, and significant investment in infrastructure.

The promise of AI in environmental sustainability is not just in its ability to process vast amounts of data or make accurate predictions. Its true value lies in its ability to help us understand the complex interconnections between different environmental systems and human activities. By illuminating these relationships, AI is helping us develop more holistic and effective approaches to environmental protection.

As we face increasingly complex environmental challenges, the role of AI in sustainability will become even more crucial. This technology offers us unprecedented tools for understanding and protecting our environment, but it's up to us to use these tools wisely and effectively. The future of environmental protection will likely depend on our ability to combine artificial intelligence with human wisdom in service of our planet's health.

The transformation of environmental protection through AI represents one of the most promising developments in our fight against climate change and environmental degradation. As these technologies continue to evolve, they offer hope that we can meet our environmental challenges with the sophistication and scale they demand.

CHAPTER 8: AI IN GOVERNANCE AND GLOBAL AFFAIRS

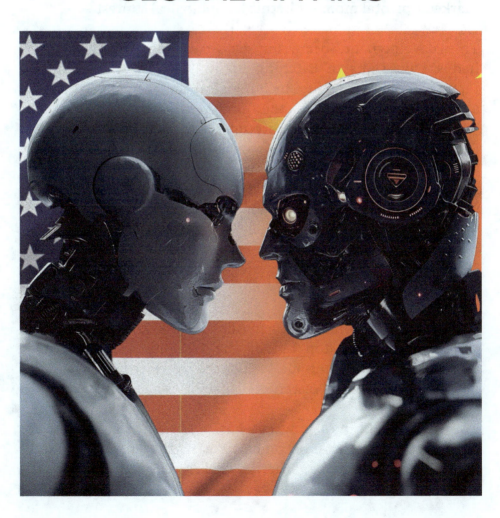

The global race for AI supremacy has intensified dramatically, fundamentally reshaping international relations and national security strategies. In a stark demonstration of this shift, China's rapid advancement in AI capabilities has sent shockwaves through the Western technological establishment. The success of Alibaba's Qwen2-VL in outperforming OpenAI's GPT-4V in several critical benchmarks marked a pivotal moment in this technological contest.

This development, occurring just two months after China had shown signs of catching up to Western AI capabilities, represents more than just technological achievement – it signals a fundamental shift in the global balance of power. The White House's response, through a comprehensive National Security Memorandum (NSM) on AI, underscores the gravity of this situation. This policy document outlines a three-pronged strategy: leading global AI development, integrating AI into national security, and establishing international governance frameworks.

The implications of this technological rivalry extend far beyond simple competition. China's success in developing advanced AI systems challenges long-held assumptions about Western technological dominance. When Alibaba's Qwen models occupied three spots in the top ten of the Hugging Face Open LLM Leaderboard, it became clear that the perceived two-year gap between Chinese and Western AI capabilities had vanished.

The speed of China's progress has particular significance for national security. As AI becomes increasingly central to military capabilities, intelligence gathering, and critical infrastructure, the stakes of this technological race continue to rise. The White

House's strategy reflects this urgency, emphasizing the need to maintain America's position as the prime destination for global AI talent while ensuring appropriate safeguards for democratic values and civil liberties.

However, this competition isn't simply binary. The global AI landscape is increasingly multipolar, with various nations developing unique approaches to AI development and governance. India's emergence as a significant player in AI research and development, Europe's focus on ethical AI frameworks, and Israel's innovations in AI security applications all contribute to a complex international ecosystem.

Government Applications

The integration of AI into governance represents one of the most significant changes in how states operate since the digital revolution. Artificial intelligence is reshaping everything from policy-making to public service delivery, promising more efficient and responsive government services while raising important questions about privacy, accountability, and democratic oversight.

Argentina's pioneering move to create an Artificial Intelligence Unit within its Cybercrime and Cyber Affairs Directorate exemplifies this transformation. The UIAAS (Artificial Intelligence Unit Applied To Security) aims to leverage AI technologies for crime prevention, detection, investigation, and prosecution. This initiative demonstrates how AI can enhance traditional government functions while raising important questions about surveillance and civil liberties.

In Buenos Aires, the AI system called Prometea has achieved a remarkable 96% success rate in predicting judicial case outcomes, significantly speeding up the drafting of housing rights-related sentences. This success illustrates AI's potential to streamline legal processes while ensuring consistent application of the law. However, it also raises critical questions about the role of human judgment in legal decision-making.

Military And Defense

The integration of AI into military operations represents perhaps the most consequential shift in warfare since the advent of nuclear weapons. Recent developments in Israel have highlighted this shift, with AI systems being deployed to identify potential targets and analyze battlefield data in real-time. The AI system known as Lavender has demonstrated unprecedented capabilities in target identification, raising both tactical possibilities and ethical concerns that demand careful consideration.

This evolution in military technology extends far beyond target identification. AI systems are now being developed to coordinate complex military operations, manage autonomous vehicles, and even predict enemy movements through pattern analysis of historical and real-time data. The implications of these developments are profound, suggesting a future where the speed of military decision-making may exceed human cognitive capabilities.

The emergence of AI in military applications has sparked an arms race of a different kind. As nations rush to develop and deploy AI-powered military systems, the traditional calculations of military power and deterrence are being rewritten. The nation that achieves superiority in military AI capabilities might gain advantages similar to those held by nuclear powers in the previous century, but with even more complex strategic implications.

However, the integration of AI into military systems presents unique challenges. Unlike traditional weapons systems, AI-powered military tools can learn and adapt, potentially in ways their creators didn't anticipate. This unpredictability introduces new risks in military planning and execution. When AI systems from opposing forces interact, the potential for rapid escalation or unexpected outcomes increases dramatically.

The ethical implications of AI in warfare cannot be overstated. The development of autonomous weapons systems raises fundamental questions about human control and accountability in military operations. The speed at which AI systems can make decisions might necessitate delegating certain military choices to algorithms, a prospect that challenges traditional notions of command responsibility and military ethics.

The future of AI in military applications will likely be shaped by the complex interplay between technological capability and ethical constraints. Nations are grappling with questions about appropriate limits on AI autonomy in military systems, the role of human oversight, and the potential for arms control agreements specific to AI capabilities. The challenge lies in harnessing the strategic advantages of military AI while preventing uncontrolled escalation or ethical breaches.

As we look to the future, the integration of AI into governance and global affairs presents both unprecedented opportunities and serious challenges. The ability to process vast amounts of data and make rapid decisions could enhance government efficiency and military effectiveness, but it also risks undermining human agency in crucial decisions about governance and warfare.

The success of nations in navigating this new landscape will depend not just on their technological capabilities, but on their ability to develop ethical frameworks and governance structures that can harness AI's potential while mitigating its risks. This requires a delicate balance between innovation and responsibility, between national advantage and global stability.

The rise of AI in governance and global affairs marks a pivotal moment in human history. We are witnessing the emergence of new forms of state power and international competition, where algorithmic capabilities may prove as important as traditional measures of national strength. The decisions made today about how to develop and deploy these technologies will shape the future of global politics and warfare for generations to come.

As AI continues to evolve, the challenge for global leaders will be to ensure that these powerful tools serve human interests and values rather than undermining them. This requires not just technological sophistication but also wisdom in establishing appropriate limits and controls. The future of governance and global security may well depend on our ability to strike this crucial balance.

The change of military and governance systems through AI is not just a technical challenge but a fundamental shift in how human societies organize and protect themselves. As we move forward, the successful integration of AI into these domains will require unprecedented levels of international cooperation, ethical consideration, and careful governance to ensure that these powerful tools enhance rather than diminish human security and well-being.

Crisis Management And Conflict Prevention

Perhaps the most promising application of AI in diplomacy lies in crisis management and conflict prevention. Advanced AI systems now monitor global events in real-time, identifying potential flashpoints before they erupt into full-scale conflicts. These systems leverage massive datasets of historical conflicts, analyzing patterns of escalation to predict potential crisis trajectories with unprecedented accuracy. By processing vast amounts of diplomatic communications, news reports, and social media data, AI can detect subtle indicators of emerging international tensions that human analysts might miss.

The United Nations and several regional organizations have embraced this technological advancement, implementing sophisticated AI-powered early warning systems. These systems continuously analyze a complex web of indicators, including social media sentiment, economic data, and political rhetoric, providing invaluable insights into potential conflict zones. When the AI detects concerning patterns, it can suggest de-escalation strategies based on successful historical precedents, giving diplomats and peacekeepers crucial time to intervene before situations deteriorate.

For example, recent deployments of these systems in regions prone to ethnic conflict have demonstrated remarkable success in predicting and preventing violent outbreaks. By identifying subtle changes in local media coverage, economic indicators, and population movements, the AI has helped peacekeeping forces position themselves strategically before tensions escalate into violence. This proactive approach represents a significant shift from traditional reactive peacekeeping methods, potentially saving countless lives through early intervention.

However, the effectiveness of these systems depends heavily on the quality and breadth of their training data. Historical biases in conflict reporting and resolution can inadvertently influence AI predictions, making it crucial to maintain diverse, globally representative datasets. Despite these challenges, the integration of AI into conflict prevention continues to evolve, offering unprecedented opportunities to maintain global peace and stability through early detection and intervention.

CHAPTER 9: THE SOCIAL IMPACT OF AI

The landscape of education is undergoing a fundamental change that extends far beyond the simple digitization of classrooms. As we look toward 2026, 2029, and beyond, artificial intelligence is reshaping not just how we teach and learn, but our very understanding of what education means in the modern world. The announcement of Eureka Labs by Andrej Karpathy marks a significant milestone in this shift. Their vision of an "AI-native" school represents more than just another technological innovation in education – it signals a fundamental shift in how we approach learning itself.

Traditional educational models, based on standardized curricula and one-size-fits-all approaches, are rapidly becoming obsolete. In their place, AI-driven personalized learning pathways are emerging, capable of adapting in real-time to each student's unique needs, interests, and learning style. This shift is particularly evident in how students engage with complex subjects like mathematics and sciences. Where once students might have struggled silently through difficult concepts, AI tutors now provide immediate, personalized feedback and alternative explanations, ensuring no student is left behind.

The role of teachers is evolving in profound ways. Rather than serving primarily as information providers, educators are becoming learning architects and mentors. They work alongside AI systems to design rich, engaging learning experiences that combine technology with human insight. In many schools, AI teaching assistants have become an organic part of the classroom ecosystem, handling routine tasks like grading and basic question-answering, freeing teachers to focus on higher-order aspects of education such as critical thinking, emotional intelligence, and creative problem-solving.

Looking ahead to 2029, the distinction between physical and virtual learning environments will become increasingly fluid. Virtual and augmented reality technologies, powered by AI, will create immersive learning experiences that make current educational technology seem primitive by comparison. Students might take virtual field trips through historic events, explore the human body from the inside, or conduct dangerous scientific experiments in completely safe, virtual environments. These aren't just simulations – they're interactive learning experiences that adapt to student responses and questions in real-time.

The shift extends to how we assess learning as well. Traditional standardized tests are giving way to continuous, AI-powered evaluation systems that measure not just knowledge retention but also critical thinking, creativity, and problem-solving abilities. These systems can track student progress across multiple dimensions, providing detailed insights into learning patterns and identifying areas where additional support might be needed. Some schools are already experimenting with "assessment-free" environments where learning progress is monitored naturally through project work and practical applications.

By 2034, we may see the emergence of fully AI-native schools where the entire learning experience is orchestrated by advanced AI systems. The concept of fixed grade levels could become obsolete, replaced by skill-based progression across various subjects. Students might seamlessly move between topics and difficulty levels, guided by AI that understands their learning patterns and goals better than any human could. This doesn't mean the elimination of human teachers, but rather a fundamental reimagining of their role in the educational process.

The integration of AI in education is also fostering a new understanding of lifelong learning. The traditional model of front-loading education in the early years of life is giving way to a more flexible, continuous approach to learning that extends throughout one's career. AI tutors can accompany individuals throughout their lives, helping them acquire new skills and knowledge as needed for personal growth or career transitions. This shift is particularly crucial in an era where technological change makes continuous learning and adaptation essential for professional success.

Mental Health And Well-Being

The intersection of AI and mental health care represents one of the most promising yet sensitive areas of technological advancement. The recent success of AI-powered mental health interventions has demonstrated the potential to democratize access to psychological support, particularly for those who might otherwise lack resources for traditional therapy. As we witness the evolution of AI systems like ChatGPT integrating sophisticated voice features and emotional recognition capabilities, we're seeing the emergence of a new paradigm in mental health support that combines accessibility with unprecedented personalization.

The latest developments in AI-assisted therapy have shown remarkable promise in addressing the global mental health crisis. In 2024, studies have demonstrated that AI systems can detect early signs of depression and anxiety through subtle changes in voice patterns, typing behavior, and daily routines – often before individuals themselves are consciously aware of their declining mental health. This predictive capability enables proactive intervention, potentially preventing the escalation of mental health issues into full-blown crises.

South Korea's new initiative with AI companion robots for seniors has become a model for addressing social isolation and loneliness. The program, which deployed over 7,000 AI robot dolls to elderly citizens living alone, has shown impressive results in improving mental well-being. These companions do more than just engage in conversation; they monitor vital signs, provide medication reminders, and even alert healthcare providers to potential concerns. The success of this program has sparked similar initiatives worldwide, with countries like Japan and Singapore developing their own versions tailored to their cultural contexts.

The technology's therapeutic applications have expanded beyond basic support. Advanced AI systems now offer specialized interventions for specific mental health conditions. For PTSD sufferers, AI-powered virtual reality exposure therapy provides carefully calibrated experiences that help patients process trauma in a controlled environment. For individuals with anxiety disorders, AI companions offer real-time coping strategies and breathing exercises, adapting their approach based on the user's physiological responses and past interactions.

However, the integration of AI into mental health care raises important ethical considerations that demand careful attention. Privacy concerns are paramount, as these systems often handle deeply personal information. There's also the risk of emotional dependency on AI systems, particularly among vulnerable populations. Mental health professionals are working to establish guidelines for appropriate AI use in therapeutic contexts, ensuring these tools enhance rather than replace human care.

The impact on professional mental health practice has been transformative. Rather than replacing human therapists, AI has become a powerful augmentation tool, helping clinicians track patient progress, identify patterns, and customize treatment plans. Some therapists now use AI assistants to handle administrative tasks and preliminary assessments, allowing them to focus more time on direct patient care. The technology also enables better coordination between different care providers, ensuring more comprehensive and consistent treatment approaches.

Perhaps most significantly, AI is helping to destigmatize mental health care. The privacy and accessibility of AI-powered support systems make it easier for people to take the first step in seeking help. Young people, in particular, have shown a greater willingness to engage with mental health resources when they can initially do so through AI interfaces. This has led to earlier intervention and better outcomes for many individuals who might otherwise have delayed seeking assistance.

Looking ahead, the integration of AI in mental health care promises even more sophisticated applications. Researchers are developing systems that can detect micro-expressions and subtle changes in body language during video calls, providing therapists with additional insights into their patients' emotional states. Work is also underway on AI systems that can understand and respond to cultural and linguistic nuances in emotional expression, making mental health support more accessible to diverse populations.

Culturally Significant In The Age Of Ai

The November 2024 Grammy nomination of The Beatles' "Now and Then" marks a watershed moment in the cultural acceptance of AI. This AI-enhanced song, featuring John Lennon's restored vocals from a 1978 demo, has been nominated for both Record of the Year and Best Rock Performance, competing alongside contemporary artists like Billie Eilish and Kendrick Lamar. The project, spearheaded by Paul McCartney, demonstrates how AI can be used to preserve and enhance cultural heritage rather than replace it. With only 78 million Spotify streams – relatively modest compared to its fellow nominees – the song's recognition speaks to the cultural significance of thoughtful AI integration in artistic creation.

The journey of "Now and Then" from a poor-quality demo to a Grammy-nominated track illustrates the evolving relationship between AI and artistic creation. The technology, initially used in Peter Jackson's "The Beatles: Get Back" documentary to separate voices from background noise, has evolved into a sophisticated tool for audio restoration and enhancement. This same technology helped producer Giles Martin create a new stereo mix for the Beatles' 1966 album "Revolver," breathing new life into classic recordings without compromising their authentic character.

Beyond music, AI's impact on cultural expression has ignited a storm across the entire artistic landscape. In visual arts, AI has evolved from basic image generation tools to become sophisticated creative collaborators, enabling artists to explore entirely new forms of expression. Museums worldwide now offer unprecedented interactive experiences where visitors can engage with AI-powered versions of historical artists or witness classical paintings spring to life, while authors and filmmakers leverage AI to enhance storytelling possibilities through interactive narratives and democratized production capabilities.

The fashion and gaming industries exemplify the most dramatic AI-driven shifts. Fashion designers harness AI not only for trend prediction but as an innovative tool for generating novel patterns and styles, while the gaming industry has achieved unprecedented levels of immersion through AI-driven characters that adapt uniquely to each player. This technological integration has given rise to entirely new art forms, from AI-human collaborative performances to virtual reality installations that dissolve traditional boundaries between artistic mediums.

CONCLUSION

We stand at a moment of unprecedented convergence in artificial intelligence. The streams of development that once flowed separately – language models, computer vision, robotics, neural interfaces – are merging into something far greater than their individual parts. This convergence manifests not just in technical capabilities, but in how AI integrates into the fabric of human experience.

The synthesis we're witnessing goes beyond simple technological integration. When Claude can analyze complex medical data while engaging in nuanced ethical discussions, when Sora can transform text into cinema-quality video while preserving artistic intent, we're seeing the emergence of systems that understand context and meaning in ways that seemed impossible just months ago.

This convergence extends into every domain of human endeavor. In healthcare, AI systems now seamlessly combine genetic analysis, medical imaging, and patient history to provide insights that no single approach could achieve. In scientific research, AI models can simultaneously process data from quantum physics experiments while suggesting novel theoretical frameworks to explain their findings. The boundaries between different types of AI capabilities are dissolving, giving rise to systems that more closely mirror the integrated way humans understand and interact with the world.

Architects Of Change

Behind every breakthrough chronicled in this volume are individuals whose vision and determination have shaped the course of AI development. Consider the story of Andrej Karpathy, whose launch of Eureka Labs represents more than just another AI education initiative – it embodies a fundamental rethinking of how humans learn and grow alongside intelligent systems.

The journey of researchers at Endiatx, who transformed the concept of swallowable robots from science fiction into medical reality, exemplifies how pioneering spirits are pushing the boundaries of what's possible. Their PillBot, navigating the human body while streaming high-resolution video, emerged from a confluence of advances in miniaturization, AI control systems, and medical imaging.

Teams at companies like Osmo aren't just developing new products – they're reimagining the very nature of human sensory experience. Their breakthrough in "scent teleportation" demonstrates how AI can help us understand and recreate aspects of human experience we once thought beyond the reach of technology.

These architects of change aren't just technologists. They include artists exploring new forms of creative expression, educators reimagining the learning process, and healthcare providers finding ways to make advanced care more accessible. Their stories remind us that the future of AI will be shaped not by algorithms alone, but by human vision and values.

The Unfinished Symphony

For all the remarkable advances we've witnessed, we're still in the early movements of AI's grand symphony. Each breakthrough reveals new horizons to explore, new challenges to overcome, new possibilities to imagine. The questions that lie ahead are as fascinating as the achievements we've documented.

What happens when AI systems become sophisticated enough to contribute to their own development? How will we navigate the enhancement of human cognitive capabilities through neural interfaces and AI augmentation? What new forms of artistic expression might emerge as AI tools become even more sophisticated creative partners?

The development of artificial general intelligence remains an open question, not just technically but philosophically. As systems like Claude demonstrate increasingly sophisticated reasoning capabilities, we must grapple with deep questions about the nature of intelligence itself.

The challenges ahead aren't just technical. How do we ensure that the benefits of AI advancement reach all of humanity? How do we maintain human agency and creativity in a world of increasingly capable artificial systems? These questions don't have simple answers, but they will shape the next chapters of AI development.

A New Chapter In Human History

As we conclude this volume, it's clear that we're not just witnessing technological progress – we're living through a fundamental transformation in human civilization. The integration of AI into every aspect of human life represents a shift as significant as the development of written language or the industrial revolution.

This transformation isn't about replacing human capabilities but expanding them. In every field we've examined, the most successful applications of AI have enhanced rather than diminished human potential. From artists finding new forms of expression to scientists making breakthrough discoveries, AI is becoming a powerful partner in human achievement.

The pace of change may seem daunting, but it also fills us with hope. We're developing tools that could help solve some of humanity's most pressing challenges, from climate change to disease. The potential for AI to enhance human understanding, creativity, and capability seems boundless.

What makes this moment truly historic isn't just the power of the technology we're developing, but the opportunity it presents to shape a better future. As we've seen throughout this volume, the most remarkable achievements have come from the synergy between human creativity and artificial intelligence.

The future belongs to those who can dance with the machines, not those who fear them. - David Borish

 This dance is just beginning, and its choreography will be written by all of us – developers and artists, scientists and educators, dreamers and doers. As we step into this new chapter of human history, we carry with us the fundamental truth that technology's greatest purpose is to enhance, not replace, the human experience.

The symphony of AI development continues to unfold, its movements echoing with both challenge and promise. Our role is not just to witness this transformation but to actively shape it, ensuring that as artificial intelligence grows more capable, human potential expands alongside it. The next chapters in this ongoing story will be written not by machines alone, but by the collective wisdom, creativity, and aspirations of humanity.

AFTERWORD

When I published the first volume of this series in April 2024, just over six months ago, I believed I had captured a pivotal moment in the history of artificial intelligence. Little did I know that the pace of innovation would accelerate so dramatically that many of the articles I had written for this second volume would require significant revision before publication. The speed of advancement in AI has been nothing short of remarkable.

This rapid evolution presents both an exciting opportunity and a humbling challenge for those of us chronicling the field. What begins as cutting-edge technology in the morning might be superseded by afternoon. The articles collected in this volume have undergone multiple revisions to keep pace with the lightning-fast developments in areas like large language models, computer vision, and artificial general intelligence.

If the first volume served as a snapshot of AI's emergence into mainstream consciousness, this second installment captures something even more profound: the moment when AI began to truly transform every aspect of human society. From healthcare breakthroughs to artistic creation, from scientific discovery to personal assistance, the applications of AI have expanded in ways that would have seemed like science fiction mere months ago.

For readers new to this series, you're joining us at an extraordinary time. The technological achievements described in these pages aren't just theoretical possibilities – they're actively reshaping our world. But more importantly, you're arriving at a moment when your voice and participation in the dialogue about AI's future have never been more crucial.

The acceleration we're witnessing brings with it new responsibilities. The ethical considerations that seemed abstract six months ago are now pressing concerns requiring immediate attention. Questions about AI safety, accountability, and equitable access have moved from academic discussions to urgent policy debates. The need for thoughtful, informed discourse about these issues has never been more critical.

I find myself simultaneously awed by the progress we've made and sobered by the magnitude of the challenges ahead. The conversations about AI's role in society must evolve as quickly as the technology itself. We need to be proactive rather than reactive, anticipating potential impacts while remaining open to unexpected possibilities.

This is why sharing knowledge and fostering dialogue about AI has become more important than ever. I encourage you to discuss these developments with others, to challenge assumptions, and to imagine possibilities. The insights you gain from these pages should serve as a starting point for deeper exploration and engagement with this transformative technology.

The pace of change shows no signs of slowing. By the time you read these words, new breakthroughs will have emerged, new questions will have arisen, and new possibilities will have opened up. This is both the challenge and the excitement of our current moment – we are all participants in one of the most significant technological transformations in human history.

As we look to the future, it becomes clear that our ability to harness AI's potential while mitigating its risks will depend on our collective wisdom and cooperation. The decisions we make today will echo through generations to come. Let this book serve not just as a chronicle of recent developments, but as a call to action – an invitation to participate in shaping the future of AI.

Together, we stand at the threshold of a new era. The coming months and years will be crucial in determining how AI technology develops and how it is integrated into our societies. Your engagement with these ideas, your participation in these discussions, and your contribution to this ongoing dialogue are more valuable than ever.

The journey continues, and it's accelerating. Let's embrace this moment of unprecedented opportunity while remaining mindful of our responsibilities to future generations. The future of AI is not predetermined – it will be shaped by the choices we make and the actions we take today.

Thank you for joining me on this extraordinary journey. May these pages inspire you to become an active participant in crafting the future of artificial intelligence.

ABOUT THE AUTHOR

David Borish

 David Borish stands at the intersection of artificial intelligence and entrepreneurial innovation, bringing nearly 25 years of experience in transforming visionary ideas into reality. As a pioneering force in AI development, he holds a significant patent (US 10,224,035) for creating the first AI Voice Search Assistant, demonstrating his early vision of AI's role in human-computer interaction.

In 2017, following Google's landmark paper on Transformer models, David and his team leveraged these innovative techniques to solve complex problems around a high-speed 360-degree camera system he had developed. The system successfully processed an unprecedented 100,000 frames in a 10-second clip.

Today, David is a sought-after keynote speaker on artificial intelligence, delivering presentations at prestigious institutions including NYU and Cornell University, where he explores AI's transformative impact on business and the creative industries. He also serves as a guest lecturer on AI at NYU Professional Studies, sharing his expertise with the next generation of innovators. As the founder and editor of "The AI Spectator" (formerly "The AI Chronicle"), he provides daily insights into the rapidly evolving AI landscape, reaching a global audience of technology enthusiasts and business leaders. His analysis and commentary have been featured in prestigious publications including Forbes Magazine, TechCrunch, Entrepreneur, and MarketWatch.

In his role as an AI Strategist, David helps organizations navigate the complex landscape of artificial intelligence, turning technological possibilities into practical business solutions. His unique approach combines deep technical knowledge with entrepreneurial acumen, enabling companies to harness AI's full potential.

Connect with David by visiting www.DavidBorish.com or @DavidBorish on your preferred social channel.

www.ingramcontent.com/pod-product-compliance
Lightning Source LLC
LaVergne TN
LVHW012332060326
832902LV00011B/1857